Unmuted

a book of ekphrastic poetry

Unmuted

a book of ekphrastic poetry

by

Nigel Kent

Nigil Kat
Sept '22

First published 2021 by The Hedgehog Poetry Press

Published in the UK by
The Hedgehog Poetry Press
5, Coppack House
Churchill Avenue
Clevedon
BS21 6QW

www.hedgehogpress.co.uk

ISBN: 978-1-913499-19-8

9 8 7 6 5 4 3 2 1

A CIP Catalogue record for this book is available from the
British Library.

for Kerry, Holly, Annie and Archie

Contents

NOMAD

after Gavin Turk

"Buy something to brighten up the drawing room," he'd said.
"Something that's a good investment too.
Maybe a Hambling, or a Hirst," he'd said,
"and not pretentious crap by some young turk."

She found it in a Bond Street gallery:
a splash of Millets' red spilled across the marbled floor.

Not quite what her husband sent her looking for...

...but only a Philistine could miss its artistry:
the soft nylon folds modelled out of painted bronze,
the sculptured zip, the foetal sleeper's silhouette,
so real she thought she smelled the stink of fetid feet,
and the sour odour of oblivion seeping from beneath.

The perfect piece! A bargain at one hundred K.
Not for the drawing room, perhaps,
better for the shadows of the portico:
a jolly jape to drop the jaws of unsuspecting guests.
A priceless double-take, a tightening of fists, then the laughter
of relief that the walls of the estate had not been breached.

MOTHER AND CHILD

after Jenny Saville

You perch on my leg,
featherless fledgling,
eager to take off.
For now I'll wrap my hands
around your naked legs,
swaddling the restlessness
that fights against my fingertips.
Yet before too long
I know you'll scorch
the air with screams,
bat away affection,
stamp on good intentions
with your sandalled feet,
...and you'll find the key
to turn the lock on me;
your ears too full of music
to hear love banging
on your bedroom door
...and you'll draw blood
with sharp remarks
that will slice and dice advice
with cold precision,
...and you'll toss my words
into cardboard boxes
like unwanted gifts, to be
abandoned in the attic.

But remember this, son,
these hands, these mother's hands,
will never stop reaching out
to break your fall.

THE PIANO LESSON

after Henri Matisse

Before the dust
had a chance to settle,
he threw the sheet
across the piano,
as if it could silence
the memories
of a son's fingers
clambering clumsily
up the scales
then stumbling down again;
of a music teacher
and a pupil out of tune;
of a boy's patience flaring
guttering, burning-out;
of the last light of day
sneaking through the window
to fetch its mate out to play;
of the metronome's wagging
finger wilfully ignored;
of the unfinished exercise
abandoned on the stand;
of a sleeping beauty
imprisoned in the instrument;
of a son who'd thrown away
the keys to set it free.

STRAIGHT

after Ai Weiwei

The clack-clack-clack of
her walking stick
disturbs
the hush
of Gallery Three,
the tired ferrule worn thin
by the labour of her steps,
made heavier by
the rucksack
riding high like a child
upon her back.

The object of
her pilgrimage:
the room-sized
fault lines
built from
the reclaimed bones
of cut-cost schools,
laid out in rows,
like the remains of
five thousand Sichaun
school children
that lined its
quake-stricken streets
seven years ago.

She stands apart
and shudders from
the aftershock that
shakes all
who've come to see
the cost of jobbery.

One hundred tons of
rebar set straight,
in remembrance of
the lives
they took.

Stooping,
she crosses
the thin red line
that keeps the public back
and lays a hand
upon the rusted steel
like a mother might
touch the face
of her stillborn child
and the room
groans
with the weight of her
grief.

THE BRONTË SISTERS

after Branwell Brontë

He scrutinises the faces
of his upright sisters
to trace exactly
the chaste lines of their lips.
He notes their eyes
are turned away;
their thoughts scudding
across a barren landscape
where feckless fools like him,
lost in the mists of wickedness
stumble from the righteous way,
their salvation sinking
in the boggy ground
beneath their wayward feet.
He knows what they are thinking -
he doesn't need to ask -
and loads his brush again,
heavy with self-loathing,
to brush out his figure and his face;
four siblings becoming three.
So much easier, he thinks,
to remedy mistakes with paint.

WOMAN WEEPING

after Pablo Picasso

Imagine a letter abandoned upon a bench
with its three respectful lines saluting
the heroic passing of an only son.

Imagine a plume of words suspended in the yard,
reeking of blood and sulphur,
that even *la tramuntana* can't disperse.

Imagine a mother driven indoors,
slamming shutters shut to silence the unkindness
of children playing soldiers in the road.

Imagine a salvo of memories
that ricochet around the room
and bring a grieving mother to her knees.

Imagine a mother praying to *la Mater Dolorosa*,
rosary beads flicking through her fingers
like bullets in a machine gun's magazine.

Imagine a miracle of bloody tears dripping
from a painted face in pity for a nation's sacrifice,
too many to mop away with a sodden handkerchief.

THE BUS RIDERS

after George Segal

She squeezes up
to make space for him,
grateful for the break
he makes from the bitter
blasts of winter air.
She feels the stranger's
warmth against her arm
against her leg,
can smell the long day's
labour through his clothes,
can even taste the lunch
of garlic ham upon his breath,
as if they were a couple,
filling the empty sofa in her flat,
where he would take
her hand and cradle it in his,
place an arm around her shoulder,
listen to her curse
the lazy landlord
who will not fix the boiler
and hear her fret
about the cut in pay
she had to take today,
but at his stop he rises,
oblivious to her shiver;
the white space between them
widening with each step;
and words, which might
have made an introduction,
remain outside, queueing
in the freezing rain.

ABOVE THE CITY

after Marc Chagall

We took a running leap
to clear the gap between us
meeting in mid-air where
I wrapped my arms around
you and perfectly attuned
we soared above their heads
not caring to look down.

We span and rolled
and looped the loop,
painted pictures in the sky,
but much too avant-garde
for the disapproving eyes
of your parents far below,
who stubbornly refused
to offer their applause.

Perhaps they heard us
laughing that the match,
between their daughter
and a lowly chap like me,
could so challenge
and confound the force
of gravity.

THE LOVERS

after René Magritte

When he came to see why
she had not answered his calls
her mother barred the door,
like a bouncer on duty
at the gates of heaven.

He saw her hiding in the hall
buttoned to the neck
with self-sacrifice,
and her guilt-ridden face caught
in a halo of sulphur-coloured light.

He'd melted her modesty
with the heat of his desire,
but now grown cold, it had set hard
like the tears of wax that gather
at the base of an altar candle.

No matter how hard she tried
her mother could not mould it
back into shape without leaving
the indelible impressions
of her fervent fingerprints.

COME TO ME

after Paula Rego

You kept your secret in the attic
harness-tight, straining
straps that proved too weak

to stop it from breaking out
and tearing away betrayal's veil
you 'd placed before my face.

Though that night I walked away
it follows me, prodding, pulling,
screaming to be appeased

and at night it breaks into my bed,
its weight so heavy on my chest
it suffocates any hope of sleep.

Yet it cannot snap the strings
which knots this heart to yours
that draw me back to where its home is.

MOBILE LOVERS

after Banksy

You wished to be like your mates
with a photo on your mantelpiece
of you smiling in the sun
with your catch held proudly in your arms,
and though you'd cast your line
and wait for the special one to bite,
at the end of the day you'd always
come home empty-handed

So you turned to the net instead,
braved deeper, murkier waters
where you watched great shoals
swim past beneath the tempered glass,
so much easier to trawl and land,
yet far too tricky to stop at one
with the endless temptation
of the next day's haul.

EVERYONE I HAVE EVER SLEPT WITH 1963-1995

after Tracey Emin

She never claimed
to be a princess
but she wasn't short of suitors
who'd bring bouquets
of promises
which always wilted overnight,
and who'd leave
a cold depression
in the sheets,
the sour smell
of disillusion stinking
out the room,
where hours before hope
had fizzed and foamed.
She doesn't run after them -
no point - but lies wasted
on her unmade bed,
craving still the crackling
surge of uncut love.

ENNUI

after Walter Sickert

She didn't marry out of love;
her happy ending
was a house with a maid
and a man of substance,
dependable as stone and gold.

She was content
to be an ornament,
delighted to be admired
from across a room
and seldom handled.

But now she gathers dust,
as her man lounges
in the parlour,
preferring the company
of gin and cigarillos.

She watches him recline,
stretching out his legs
across the hours,
tripping up time,
and blocking its passing.

He's blinded by indifference
that smoulders
as she tries to speak,
its smoke spiralling
from his untroubled lips

and its ashes falling to his feet,
which he'll grind into the rug
like the remnants of her hopes,
when he deigns to take his leave,
and locks her once again in silence.

AUTOMAT

after Edward Hopper

In the lull
after the rush
she follows his plan
to the final letter,
X.
She takes her seat
at the empty table
near the exit.
Tick!
Hat and coat on,
ready for the getaway.
Tick!
Back to the window,
to frustrate the prying
eyes of passers-by.
Tick!
Right glove off,
to hold the cup,
left glove on,
to hide her lie.
Tick!
The crumbs of apple pie,
the perfect alibi.
Tick!
She waits.
Tick! Tick! Tick!

Sipping away
the minutes,
lips still tasting
of the bitterness
of this morning's Judas kiss.
Tick!
She listens
for the serpent
hiss of tyres,
Tick!
hears the muffled thump
of a taxi door,
Tick!
and feels his hand on hers
pulling her away
into December's darkness.

WOMAN IN BLUE READING A LETTER

after Jan Vermeer

The long-awaited letter
finally arrives
with its paucity of words,
as if he'd had to pay
for them with gold.

He lands tomorrow,
in a ship whose hold
boasts of New World pelts,
that will soon bedeck
the head of every man
in Amsterdam.

But nothing else.

No sentiments.

All mutinous words
he'd cast adrift,
lest they testify
to the terms
of their relationship:
the deal he'd sealed
to trim ambition's
costly sails,
set on a course
to leave her
forever on the quay,
clutching a handkerchief,
the ledger closed.

THE AWAKENING CONSCIENCE

after William Holman Hunt

She knew   it wouldn't be   the ring   inside the tissue-covered box.   It was
a small oak case instead with   the copper-coloured butterfly he'd
caught,displayed inside: its delicate wings outstretched.   She thought it still
might   fly   were it not for the silver pin   fixing   it to the silken bed
beneath.   She placed it with his other trinkets   in the gaudy chest of drawers
and let him pull her down onto his lap;   as captive for his song.   His fingers
stroked the sentimental music from the keys,   and something fluttered   in
the abandoned cavern of her heart: something she feared smothered many
months ago   when he trapped her   with his net of promises and lies.   A
shaft of light had   burst   into the room to set the shadows   free   and lit
a passage to the window,   where with shawl stretched out,   like a pair of
ruddy wings,   she rose up   into the summer sky.

LE VIOLON D'INGRES

after Man Ray

His hands modelled me,
folding my arms forward
smoothing them out of sight,
accentuating my contours,
before the bristles of his brush
traced the shape of the f-holes
on the sound box of my back.
A joke to please his arty friends:
Ingres' bather as a naked violin.
For six years I was happy to be
his bare-backed Stradivarius
and for him to be my virtuoso,
making mellow music every day
and I resounded to his touch.
Till his playing turned clumsy
from familiarity then neglect.
A friction grew between us
that turned me sharp and shrill,
and we fell out of tune,
so we could play no more,
and I grieved deeply, longing for
his fingers' touch upon my neck,
for he'd found in me a resonance
that was both rich and deep
which must be heard again.

WAITING (THE CHAPERONE)

after Edgar Degas

Black dress, black coat,
black hat, black shoes:
it was if she was in mourning
for a life that had passed.

The Chaperone, a shadow
on the bench in *le foyer de la danse,*
ignored by the half-naked dancers,
who fluttered past her.

Observer of their lesson:
of his hand upon a hip,
of his finger lifting a chin,
of his hot breath upon a neck,

watching the girls acquire
the moves she could never master;
for she was never flexible enough
to earn the pleasure of the *abonnés.*

STAG AT STARKEY'S

after George Bellows

From our ringside seats
we watch him
bouncing lightly on his feet,
striking with his cobra-right,
and glowing brightly in the lights,
as if blessed by some divinity.
He vanquishes adversaries
only we can see;
opponents that leave
us lesser men lying
limp upon the canvas,
the blood-stained towel
thrown in.
How we cheer
each punch he lands
that doubles up
our grasping landlords,
that brings our penny-pinching
bosses to their knees,
that sends our lying leaders
reeling around the ring,
and when the ref steps in
to raise the winner's arm,
he sends us home
a little richer,
a little more erect,
wishing our kids asleep
and our wives awake,
awaiting our victorious return.

THE ART CRITIC

after Raoul Hausmann

He circles the gallery,
stooping towards the work,
face inches from the canvas,
like some enormous hound
sniffing at what he's found
and looking as though he might
at any moment lift a leg
to pass his judgment on a piece.
Except he's too genteel for that.
Believes himself a man of standards
the ultimate curator of taste,
defender of the gullible
against the march of the avant-garde
with words sharpened on tradition's steel.
He dreams that with the deftest strokes
he'll drive these soulless anarchists
from culture's lofty barricades,
for God forbid, if not stopped,
they threaten to befoul
the greatest beauties of the past
with painted beards and black moustaches.

PORTRAIT OF SYLVIA VON HARDEN

after Otto Dix

She sits alone at a table
in the baby-pink corner of the club;
irony painted on her face.

Her monocled eye censures
the simpering women draped round
the necks of men like pale silk scarves.

Her hair, unlike theirs, is grateful
it's been spared the tongs' coercion
into forelock-touching curls

and her figure celebrates
its freedom from the stays that squeeze
her sisters' waists into submission.

She drinks a strong Martini
and draws upon a Russian cigarette,
savouring the smoky taste of revolution.

Later she will dance alone,
moving to the emancipated rhythms
beating wildly in her head,

the volume so loud it silences
the boots marching in the street,
summoned to protect the ceiling made of glass.

HIM

after Maurizio Cattelan

We saw him
through the bars
of the gates
on Prozna Street,
at the broken heart
of the Warsaw ghetto,
where seventy years before
families and friends,
like bags of the city's waste,
were bundled into trucks
bound for Treblinka's ovens.
A diminutive figure
in a woollen,
knickerbocker suit,
and scuffed, brown boots,
on his knees,
as if overcome
by the faecal stink
of despair that
after all these years
still seems to linger
in the city's air.
So easy to mistake
him for a penitent
or a child,
were it not for
the slick of black hair,
the toothbrush moustache,
the Final Solution.

AMERICAN GOTHIC

after Duncan Wood

We said he looked like a banker
with his round-lensed glasses,
close-cut balding pate
and black woollen jacket
hiding the bib and brace beneath.
His hands, though, told a different story:
skin as rough as bark, horn-hard,
weathered by the daily toil
that stalled our loan's foreclosure.

When the Depression scorched
the State and cash was as sparse
as water on our land,
he did not seek salvation
in the loaded chamber of a gun,
like the broken city bankers.
He rose earlier still, well before dawn,
to tend the survivors in our stock
and feed them with unfailing Faith.

He'd not return till nightfall,
wearing a coat of dust and sweat
hungry for his grits and greens.
Afterwards we'd sit upon the porch,
fatigue bankrupting conversation,
his face turned towards the heavens
in the growing gloom, finding
God's eternal grace and bounty
in the promise of the stars.

GIRL AT THE MIRROR

after Norman Rockwell

No matter how much she pouted
the mirror would not tell her
that she was the fairest of them all:
she was just an ordinary girl
with ordinary looks,
more painted doll, than movie star.

Not like the other girls her age
who with dabs of rouge upon their cheeks
could blush encouragement to the boys
and who could shape their uninviting lips
into the crimson promise of a kiss.
So why, oh why, couldn't she?

Her mother wouldn't show her,
protected her from the bare-faced truth
of all those yawning hours
spent behind the bathroom door,
fashioning different fantasies
to keep her husband loyal.

Despite her pleas she would not teach her
those painted lies women hide behind
or tell her of the day she could no longer
find her self reflected in the mirror,
for she'd disappeared forever
in those puffs of perfumed powder.

UNTITLED FILM STILL #27

after Cindy Sherman

Action. He blocks her way, requests a light calls her 'Love'. She doesn't know him yet she'd met his sort before: the balding office boss whose gaze brazenly invades her space; the harassed family man who brushes hard against her on the rush-hour bus; the bar-room businessman who demands a generous return on the investment of a drink. She watches the stranger's tongue flick out to lick his lips savouring her nervousness. She strikes a match to see him off. His hand coils round hers squeezing squashing crushing and as he leans towards the flame his pupils flare and she sees the fire raging in the pit. She feels its heat upon her face her skin burning bubbling melting into a liquid as clear as tears that settles in a steaming puddle at his snakeskin shoes over which he lightly skips to saunter down the indifferent street chest out a thin stream of smoke escaping through his fang-like teeth. *Cut.*

L'ABSINTHE

after Edgar Degas

Monsieur Patron,
how inviting you look
in your emerald finery,
Come! Let me taste
your promise on my lips
No holding back.

Come! Slip off
the shame of my trade in
one franc fantasies.
Unbutton my misery;
let it fall to my feet
like a soiled petticoat.

Take me to that private place
where clarity is clouded,
where we dissolve,
and where you fill me
with that bitter sweetness
till I can take no more.

Let me feel again
the comforts of numbness,
hear the symphony of silence,
see the beauty of blindness
until you must turn your back
to snuff the candle out.

THIRD-CLASS CARRIAGE

after Honoré Daumier

He positions her in the centre
of the canvas, a grandmother,
framed by her widowed daughter
and her two grandchildren,
bound for the last resort of the city
in the jolting, jarring carriage.
The light illuminates her face
as if she were a haloed saint
painted by some renaissance great,
except there is no rapture here,
just a face chiselled by hardship,
its features abraded by the daily grind,
and though her hands,
resting on the basket's handle,
look as though they're locked in prayer,
her eyes aren't turned towards the heavens
but fixed upon the journey's end instead:
the final stop from which
she knows she won't return.
Until then she will not rest
but bear the weight of her daughter
and her children without complaint:
a modest third-class sort of martyrdom
of days of downcast eyes and open hands,
of the evening sacrifice of meals,
of nights shivering under the blanket of shadows,
out of view of the Minister dozing peacefully
in the upholstered comfort of first class.

HEAD OF A MINER

after Josef Herman

This man doesn't hit the headlines;
he doesn't have a chiselled chin;
or slicked back, Brylcreemed hair,
or teeth that dazzle when he smiles.
You won't find him marching on parades
with rows of medals glinting in the sun
or see adoring women falling at his feet.
He wears instead a uniform of grime
to battle long and hard, unseen,
deep beneath the Valleys' fields
to liberate the coal trapped underground.
His medals are the back-slaps of his mates,
and the kisses of a wife who listens
for the scrape of boots upon the step
to brush away the vestiges of dread
and check her welcome in the mirror
before she asks him how his day has been,
knowing he will not tell her
about the crumbling ceiling of the drift,
or the gas they found seeping from the face,
or about the cough he's suffered from
for months but cannot seem to shake.

AN IRON FORGE

after Joseph Wright

A sound from the old forge
that the villagers hadn't heard before,
louder than cannon and mortar,
a pounding that makes
the ground tremor,
the chimneys tremble,
shakes rats from the thatches,
and spills the poor from their beds
who peer from windows
fearing the second coming.
But this isn't gospel prophecy
more Mammon's manifesto.
This is the rhythm of a revolution
that has rallied the elements to its cause.
This is the might of fire,
the force of flood, unleashed,
that drive the village labourers
to find asylum in distant city's streets.
This is the alchemy
of leather-aproned blacksmith
turned waist-coated industrialist:
the manufacture of a capitalist,
who leads the march of machinery,
his mighty trip hammer beating out time,
as each resounding blow
fashions base metal into gold.

COMING FROM THE MILL

after L.S. Lowry

They spill out
of the mill gates,
heads bowed,
shoulders stooped,
as if beaten
into homage
to the might
of the machines
that they must serve:
those iron tyrants
that dictate their days,
that censor conversations,
that turn their thoughts to lint
that will exact a scalp
or a careless finger
for every lapse
in concentration.
Too tired to talk,
the workers walk alone -
silent, divided, conquered.
No union of comrades
permitted here,
no red flags
to rally round
only the white cotton
flag of surrender.

CHRISTINA'S WORLD

after Andrew Wyeth

She wasn't running away;
since the illness
laid waste to her legs
she couldn't run,
but she'd crawled
and rolled much further
than she'd thought.
Far enough
to feel stranded
in this sea of grass.
To save herself,
her slender arms
must pull her home:
against the rising tide
of meadow-waves,
her legs, like anchors,
slowing her passage
across the gulf
that stretches between
her and the house,
bobbing on the horizon,
always one step
out of reach.

OPHELIA

after John Everett Millais

This isn't a picture
of a young girl
caught in a current of insanity,
dragged under
its churning surface
flailing helplessly
as she's dashed against
the rocks of loss and grief
that lurk beneath.
No, this is altogether different:
this is a girl seduced by suicide,
the charmer, the smooth-talker,
who whispers in her ear,
professing he can feel her pain,
and promises he can save her
from her endless suffering.
In gratitude she parts her lips
in preparation for his kiss,
reaches out her arms,
inviting him to take her hand
to lead her to the water's edge
where it is deep enough
to drown despair
and guarantee the peace she seeks.
She does not hesitate
but steps into its depths
to lay her head upon the river's bed
and sink into eternal sleep.

ETERNITY'S GATE

after Vincent Van Gogh

He pulls his chair
towards the fire
as if the flames
might thaw the blizzard
of regrets and fears
that buries words
without a trace.
He sits, shivering,
with head in hands
and rocks to the rhythm
of a silent lullaby
that melts the ice-hard knots
of eighty years
and sets him free
to bathe in dreams,
that dissolve time
until he must rise
to the rattle
of Eternity's gate
its frozen latch,
released.

RESOURCES

To view the art works that inspired these poems visit:

https://nigelkentpoet.wordpress.com/unmuted/

and click on the links.

ACKNOWLEDGEMENTS

This collection would never have been written without the support and friendship of Stephen Belinfante, Nick Browne and John Prangnell and without our many trips to galleries in London, Birmingham and Bristol which allowed me to experience in such knowledgeable company so many of the artworks that inspired these poems.

My gratitude to the members of The Open University Society of Poets, who in our Zoom sessions over the last twelve months have listened to early drafts of the poems and provided valuable encouragement and feedback.

Finally my eternal thanks to Mark Davidson, Editor of Hedgehog Press, for his continuing faith in my work and willingness to publish it.